DAVID COLBERT

10
DAYS

THOMAS EDISON

ALADDIN PAPERBACKS

NEW YORK LONDON TORONTO SYDNEY

❧ ALADDIN PAPERBACKS • An imprint of Simon & Schuster Children's Publishing Division • 1230 Avenue of the Americas, New York, NY 10020 • Copyright © 2008 by David Colbert • All rights reserved, including the right of reproduction in whole or in part in any form. • ALADDIN PAPERBACKS and related logo are registered trademarks of Simon & Schuster, Inc. • Cover designed by Karin Paprocki • Interior designed by David Colbert • Special thanks to Paul Gasbarra and Jesse Waters for their significant contributions to this book, and to John Chew for his mathematical expertise. • The text of this book was set in Perpetua. • Manufactured in the United States of America • First Aladdin Paperbacks edition September 2008 • Library of Congress Control Number 2008920646 • ISBN-13: 978-1-4169-6444-5 • ISBN-10: 1-4169-6444-4 • 10 9 8 7 6 5 4 3 2 1

CONTENTS

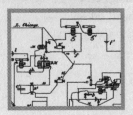

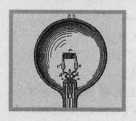

INTRODUCTION

I n an age when ships and trains ran on steam, Thomas Edison was building an early version of the Internet. He was wiring the world when that meant actually climbing on rooftops to run the wires. This was even before electrical power plants existed. You couldn't plug an appliance into a wall outlet, because there were no outlets. Everything ran on crude, acid-filled batteries. Yet Edison's inventions will seem familiar to anyone who uses the Internet today. He pioneered text messaging, making it possible for multiple messages to be sent at once, just as today's computers do. Later he added voice technology. Then, while trying to invent voice mail, he came up with portable music. A few years afterward he created a popular video-clip player that works on the same principle as YouTube—in fact, some of the video clips he created can be seen on YouTube today.

Somewhere in the middle of all this he invented the lightbulb.

If Edison were alive now he'd be running a company in Silicon Valley. The research and engineering systems he developed became admired models for business. He knew how to deal with venture capitalists and the stock market. He was brilliant at publicity. He also knew what Microsoft, Apple, and every other successful Silicon Valley company of today knows: how to improve a competitor's idea and turn a laboratory theory into a must-have gadget.

Most of the best-known photographs of Edison

show him as an old man with gray hair, creating a false impression of a grandfatherly tinkerer. Actually, he was young during his most creative period. He was in his early twenties at the time of his first success, and just over thirty when the lightbulb was invented. He attacked every project with intense drive. In all-night sessions at his laboratory, he would think of dozens or even hundreds of possible solutions to the problem at hand, then he and his assistants would try each one. He was a lot like young people today who have always lived in a wired world and understand the new technology better than many adults. The same generation gap existed in his time. He was the Boy Wonder.

Over the course of his life, technology exploded. When he was born in 1847, railroads and the telegraph were new. If you wanted to travel fast or get a message to someone quickly, your best choices were horseback or riverboat. If you were an inventor, you had to make most of your parts by hand. If you were making an electrical gadget, you had to create your own electrical power. When Edison wanted to bring electric light to New York City, he had to build the country's first power station. But by the time Edison died in 1931, there was photography, motion pictures, the telephone, the airplane, the automobile, the X-ray, air-conditioning, television, all sorts of appliances— and the world was lit with electric light.

"Genius is one percent inspiration, ninety-nine percent perspiration," he said. He certainly was not an accidental success. He had enormous ambition. Sometimes, however, that ambition propelled him far along a course he should have abandoned. Because he was essentially self-educated and self-made, and had achieved great success, he tended to trust his instincts even when evidence suggested he was wrong. This led to trouble a few times. He missed some great opportunities for his discoveries. He refused to acknowledge better technology created by certain competitors. He sometimes cut ethical corners.

Still, most of the 30,930 days he lived were filled with fascinating attempts at discovery and invention that foreshadow the most modern inventions of the electronic age. Here are the ten days that changed his world—and yours.

1 2 3 4 5 6 7
8 9 → 10 ← 1 2 3
4 5 6 7 8 9 10 1 2
3 4 5 6 7 8 9 10 1 2
3 4 5 6 7 8 9 10

ONE TWO THREE FOUR FIVE SIX

DAY 1

FALL,
1862

ONE

BUILT FOR SPEED

Mt. Clemens, Michigan.

O n this fall day—historians aren't sure of the exact date, although Edison and two of the other people present remained friends for the rest of Edison's life—fifteen-year-old Tom Edison is at the train station in this Great Lakes town. A train station is where Edison is happiest. It's where he's connected to the rest of the world. Starting just a few years before Edison's birth on February 11, 1847, and continuing through his childhood, two breakthroughs in technology, the railways and the tele-graph, have been creating an international network of people and ideas.

The whole world isn't wired yet. Most people still travel on foot or horseback or by boat. For many Americans, canals and rivers are more important than roads. Faster, too. But for people who are near a rail-way station or a telegraph office, the whole world seems within reach.

Adults are having trouble keeping up with the changes. For Edison's generation, each step forward is natural, easy, and thrilling.

This new era began for Edison when the Grand Trunk Railway, a Canadian line, reached his town of Port Huron, Michigan, three years earlier. The line runs all the way east to the Atlantic Ocean, hundreds of miles away. Because it runs a daily train of European immigrants traveling from eastern seaports to the Midwest, more new faces—and new ideas—pass through Port Huron in a day than a resident would

The western half of the Grand Trunk Railway

have encountered in a year before the railway arrived.

Moving even faster than the trains are the clicks on the new telegraph lines that run alongside the tracks. Although the telegraph is only a few years older than Edison himself, it has already changed the world. By tapping out messages in a combination of short and long signals—"dots" and "dashes"—telegraph operators relay text messages from station to station through the network, just like a modern-day e-mail or

Thomas Edison at age 14. Family and friends called him "Al," which was short for his middle name, Alva.

text message is passed from one computer server to another until it reaches its destination.

Because the relaying is done by operators rather than machines, the speed is slower than what we expect over the Internet; but compared to what existed before the telegraph, the change is more astonishing than what the Internet brought to the modern era. Four years before this day, mail between the eastern United States and California could take months to reach its destination. A year earlier, the transcontinental telegraph was completed, and now a message can cross the country in hours.

Every day the telegraph network grows. Local networks all over the world are being linked together. Four years earlier, when Edison was eleven, the world witnessed the nineteenth-century equivalent of putting astronauts on the moon: A telegraph cable was laid across the Atlantic Ocean to link Europe with North America. Queen Victoria of Great Britain and U.S. President James Buchanan exchanged messages, and both countries had huge celebrations with parades and fireworks. Britain already has short undersea cables to France and the Netherlands, linking it to a network that spreads across Europe. Undersea cables are being prepared to link Arabia with India, and China with Australia. (In modern times, Internet traffic runs along cables that follow many of the same routes as these original telegraph lines.)

> **ALTHOUGH THE FIRST TRANSATLANTIC CABLE WAS DAMAGED SOON AFTER COMPLETION, A REPLACEMENT CABLE WAS SUCCESSFULLY CONNECTED IN 1866.**

Text messaging via telegraph has already changed the Civil War, which has been underway for about a year. President Abraham Lincoln has more control over his field officers than any president before him. He gets news from the field in time to direct an immediate response, and with his generals in Washington he can coordinate parts of the army that don't have direct communication with one another.

Songs were written to celebrate the completion of the 1858 transatlantic telegraph cable. This one is dedicated to Cyrus W. Field, head of the company that undertook the challenge.

His telegraph messages—one historian cleverly calls them "t-mails"—are essential to the Union's efforts. He's even learned to change his writing style to adapt to the technology. Instead of long instructions, he sends short, punchy text messages.

In this regard, Lincoln is the exception. For the most part, even those adults who make use of the railways and telegraph don't truly understand them. They rely on people like Edison—younger people for

An 1869 map of existing and proposed
telegraph routes that link the continents

whom the technology is perfectly normal. Edison is happy to oblige. Although he's still a young teenager, Edison is already a businessman.

ON THE MOVE

A few years earlier Edison's mother began teaching him at home, which has helped him develop confidence and his natural independent streak. The little time he spent at the local school wasn't as successful as her lessons. Some stories blame his schoolteacher, but other reasons are more likely. His curiosity led him to ask a lot of questions and pursue subjects in his own way. He was also partially deaf, which made it difficult for him to follow lessons.

In later years, Edison told a couple of stories to explain how he became deaf. In one it happened when he was lifted onto a train by his ears. In another his head was slapped by an angry conductor after a problem on a train. Doctors now say the real reason may be one or more of the many illnesses he suffered as a child, which included scarlet fever. Whatever the cause, Edison refuses to let the condition slow him down. If anything, it makes him more determined and focused.

By the time he was twelve, he has convinced his mother to let him work on the railroad, selling newspapers and snacks to the passengers. Each day he rides to Detroit and back. The trip is three hours in each direction, with a stop in the city of several hours. In Detroit, Edison spends the time reading at the library or coming up with new business ideas. One of his better ideas is to buy fruits, vegetables, butter, and jam from farmers along the route and in shops in Detroit, so he can sell them on the train and in Port Huron. Business is so good he hires other boys to help.

Sometimes, however, his curiosity runs a little wild. He's interested in chemistry, another field that's going through an important era of new discovery. He puts together a chemistry set and keeps it on a shelf in a baggage car so he can experiment when he's not busy. One day a bottle of phosphorus sets the baggage car on fire! (This is when he gets slapped by the conductor. Fortunately, no one else was hurt.)

Mostly, however, it's the telegraph that fascinates him. He instinctively understands how it's changing the world. He has already set up a private telegraph line, almost a mile long, between his house and the house of a friend.

One spring day in 1862, as the train pulls into the Detroit station, Edison sees a huge crowd in front of a bulletin board. Everyone's panicked by news reports that tens of thousands of soldiers have been killed or wounded in the Battle of Shiloh, the largest battle in American history to that time. Edison persuades the telegraph operator to send the news down the telegraph line to all the stations between Detroit and Port Huron. He knows it'll spread through every town by the time the evening train leaves Detroit. Then he races to the office of the Detroit Free Press, for which he usually sells a hundred newspapers a day, and asks for a thousand copies. The publisher thinks he's crazy at first, but Edison explains to him what it means to have telegraphed the news along the railway line: Crowds will be waiting at each station to buy the newspaper when the train stops. Edison gets his papers, and he's right about the crowds. Every copy of the paper is gone by the time he gets home that night. He created a flash mob!

Shortly afterward he gets another idea that appears to come from the future. More than a century and a quarter before portable computers and printers are invented, he takes a very small "proofing" press, designed for checking a single page of type before the type gets added to the rest of a newspaper or book, and turns it into a laptop printer for a newspaper that he publishes right on the train. The *Grand Trunk Herald* is aimed at employees of the railway: It has news, gossip, announcements, and Edison's own opinions. He soon has a few hundred subscribers.

ACTIONS AND WORDS

N ow on this cool fall day Edison is inside one of the stations on the route to Detroit. He's become so successful that other boys now work on the trains for him. He spends most days watching the telegraph operators along the route and looking for chances to practice.

The skills needed to send a message are different from the skills needed to receive one. You can send at your own pace, but you have to receive at the pace of the operator on the other end of the line. Harder still, you have to mentally translate those dots and dashes into letters. This is like using binary computer code to communicate on a computer.

In fact, Morse code has a lot in common with

the computer codes that run the Internet. Morse is a binary code, meaning it uses various combinations of just two symbols—a dot and a dash—to signify each letter of the alphabet. "A," for example, is a dot followed by a dash, which is transmitted on a telegraph line as a short signal followed by a long one. Computer codes are also binary when you get down to the level used by the machine itself. In the first ASCII computer language developed at the time the Internet was being built, the letter "A" is a series of ones and zeroes—"100 0001" to be exact.

You don't worry about writing binary code when you type an e-mail or a text message. You type "A" and the machine does the rest. Then the machine on the other end translates the code back into the letter "A" before displaying it. But in the early days of the telegraph there were no machines to translate words into Morse code and back again. The operator did it.

Morse code is hard to master. Edison needs to practice receiving from real operators. Because most

This was an early "key" used to tap text messages in Morse code.

are too busy to help, he's not progressing as quickly as he'd like.

Today he's practicing at the Mt. Clemens station, sitting next to the operator and trying to keep up with a message that's being received. Then there's a low rumble underneath his feet. A train's coming into the station. He instinctively looks out the window, and his eyes open wide: There's a child crawling around on the tracks—the son of the man who runs the train station, James MacKenzie.

The telegraph operator is so busy sending his message that he doesn't notice. Springing from his chair, Edison runs into the yard and scoops the small boy off the track just before the train arrives.

Across the yard, on the other side of the tracks, the boy's mother has witnessed the near-catastrophe. She shrieks and then faints. Workmen come running and quickly figure out what's happened. Someone sends for the station manager to help his wife.

By the time James MacKenzie arrives, his wife has been revived. She tells her husband the whole story: She'd just turned her back for a second, and when she turned around again the boy was on the tracks and Edison was pulling him from harm's way.

MANY ABBREVIATIONS USED IN TEXT MESSAGES TODAY WERE ALSO USED BY MORSE CODE OPERATORS. A FEW OF THEM:

CUL: SEE YOU LATER
GG: GOING
SEZ: SAYS
TNX: THANK YOU
U: YOU
UR: YOU ARE
88: LOVE AND KISSES

A grateful MacKenzie offers Edison some money as a reward. Edison refuses it. But he does ask if MacKenzie would be willing to do him a favor. Would MacKenzie teach him how to operate the telegraph like a professional? MacKenzie agrees.

Edison's life immediately takes a great shift. He focuses only on the telegraph, and with MacKenzie's help, he's soon ready to strike out on his own.

Many years later, after Edison has not only mastered the new technology but reshaped it, Edison will hire both MacKenzie and his son. They'll all share fond memories of the days back in their little station. Neither the senior MacKenzie nor Edison will ever forget the day they changed each other's lives. **❶**

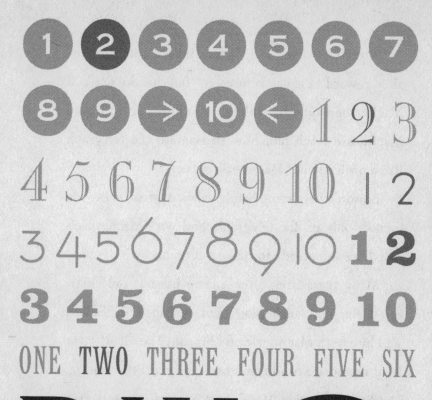

ONE **TWO** THREE FOUR FIVE SIX

DAY 2

TWO

———————————

JANUARY 30,

1869

NETWORKING

Boston.

Edison usually doesn't notice the arrival of the morning mail. Today, however, he anxiously gets up from his notebooks every few minutes and looks out the window to see if the mail carrier is coming. He has placed an ad in *The Telegrapher*, a magazine published by the telegraph operators' union, and wants to see how it looks.

The ad isn't for a product. It's for Edison himself. He's announcing that he's quitting the job he wanted so much when he was a fifteen-year-old in Michigan. After more than six years as a telegraph operator, he's had some extraordinary adventures and has made a name for himself in the industry. Now almost twenty-two, he has something even bigger planned.

ROAD WARRIOR

After Edison saved the young son of James MacKenzie, the grateful father made good on his promise to teach Edison telegraphy and Morse code. Then the telegraph operator at the Port Huron Station left to join the Union Army, and Edison was given a part-time position to replace him. It was the first of a series of jobs all over North America: Stratford Junction, Ontario, Canada; Adrian, Michigan; Fort Wayne, Indiana; Indianapolis, Indiana; Cincinnati, Ohio; Memphis, Tennessee; Louisville, Kentucky; New Orleans, Louisiana; and Boston, Massachusetts. He bounced around for five years, sometimes going back to a city where he'd worked before, but mostly looking for something new.

He was a young man in a hurry, but he was getting nowhere fast. At one point he almost moved to Brazil after reading an advertisement for telegraph jobs there. He changed his mind at the last minute because of an encounter with a stranger in the steamship office. After mentioning that he was moving to Brazil for work, he got some advice that he remembered years later.

Library of Congress

The young telegrapher

"I've sailed the seas for fifty years," the man said, "and have been in every port in every country, and there's no country like the U.S. If there's anything in a man, the U.S. is the place to bring it out. Any man who leaves this country to better his condition is an ignorant damned fool."

Edison had been having last-minute doubts, and the man's strong advice changed his mind. The man was right, even though a lot of the country was in turmoil following the Civil War. (In New Orleans, where the conversation took place, there had just been a race riot and a massacre of African Americans. Edison also saw racial violence in Memphis and Louisville.) Despite its many problems at the time, the United States still offered more opportunities than South America or Europe for a man like Edison.

THE INCIDENT IN NEW ORLEANS ON JULY 30, 1866, WAS AN ATTACK AGAINST PROTESTORS WHO WERE CHALLENGING NEW LOCAL LAWS MEANT TO LIMIT THE RIGHTS OF AFRICAN AMERICANS. IT DREW NATIONAL ATTENTION. THERE WERE CONCERNS THE WAR WOULD START AGAIN.

Considering his later success, Edison's real problem may be surprising: For a long time, he was bad at his job. He was unable to send or receive messages at the speeds achieved by first-rate telegraphers. Also, he didn't give his full attention to his work. He preferred to tinker with new devices and methods that would improve the young technology. Although he chose night shifts so he could do his experiments or read scientific books and journals, his bad habits were noticed. After almost causing a deadly train crash at a job in Canada, he came close to being arrested. Before the head of the railway could call the police, Edison slipped away and caught the first train leaving Toronto for the United States.

MOTHER OF INVENTION

While he wasn't much of a telegraph operator, he was brilliant in his understanding of the medium. His inventions were all meant to push telegraphy from what it was to what it could be. To make it easier for operators to receive messages that came over the line quickly, he adapted a machine that recorded the Morse code signals on paper to also play back the signals at a slower speed. Going a step further, he created a printer that could automatically type out messages as they were received. For a company trying to sell telegraphs in China, he tried to create a fax machine so users could send handwritten Chinese characters. (The closest thing to a fax machine at the time was a device that used a nine-foot-tall pendulum. Faxes wouldn't be common in offices until the mid-1980s.) He also came up with devices to improve how signals traveled along telegraph lines. A signal can lose its strength over the course of about twenty miles. It requires boosters along the way and automatic relays to send it to the right place. Edison made those too.

Edison was making the same kind of improvements to the telegraph network that engineers would make to computers and the Internet a century later: He was making information move along the network faster and farther, and he was improving what we now call the "interface"—the human interaction with the machine. He was like Steve Jobs and Steve Wozniak in the early days of Apple Computer, trying to make the technology so easy anyone could use it. He didn't want the telegraph operator to adjust to the telegraph; he wanted the machine to adjust to the operator. The first practical typewriters had only just been introduced while he was working on a device that would let an operator with no knowledge of Morse code send a message by using a dial to select actual letters of the alphabet. In essence this was an early electric keyboard. (The dial ran from *A* to *Z*. The QWERTY configuration of horizontal keyboards hadn't been invented yet.)

INDEPENDENCE DAY

Now Edison lives in Boston, where he has been working at the Western Union telegraph office. Thanks to friends he has made in the past few years, and to articles he has published in *The Telegrapher*, he has earned a good reputation and the trust of businessmen who finance his inventions.

Always keen to earn money, he has also been setting up private telegraph lines for companies that have more than one location in the city. In Edison's time, that meant climbing to the roofs of buildings to stretch wires across the city, and attaching all the power supplies and boosters and relays the system needed. Only then could he could attach the terminals that were actually used to send and receive messages. He also set up a service that would become very important to him later: the delivery of stock and gold prices via telegraph. Banks and brokerage firms in Boston are eager to receive the latest prices from the floor of the stock and gold exchanges in other cities, like New York.

His success has given him the confidence to leave behind the relatively simple work of sending and receiving messages as an operator for Western Union. He already has a notebook full of good ideas. Today he's going to act on them.

Finally, the mail! Edison quickly flips through the pages of *The Telegrapher* and finds the advertisement he placed. With a smile on his face, he reads the announcement: "*Mr. T. A. Edison has resigned his situation in the Western Union office, Boston, and will devote his time to bringing out his inventions.*" ②

① ② ③ ④ ⑤ ⑥ ⑦

⑧ ⑨ → ⑩ ← 1 2 3

4 5 6 7 8 9 10 1 2

3 4 5 6 7 8 9 10 **12**

3 4 5 6 7 8 9 10

ONE TWO **THREE** FOUR FIVE SIX

DAY 3

DECEMBER 30,

1874

T
H
R
E
E

ALL THAT GLITTERS

New York City.

No matter how hard he tries, Edison can't get a smile out of the man visiting his laboratory. Jay Gould, one of the most famous businessmen in America and also one of the most hated, isn't in the mood for any of the jokes Edison loves to tell. He only wants to see Edison's latest invention, which could revolutionize the world's telegraph networks.

The meeting is secret. Edison has already promised

the device to one of Gould's competitors. However, in the bare-knuckle world of nineteenth-century business, that doesn't count for a lot. Making a last-minute bid for this invention would be nothing compared to what Gould has done in the past few years. Using his position as head of the Erie Railroad Company, he manipulated the stock price to make huge profits. About five years earlier, he and some partners caused a panic in the financial markets with an audacious scheme to manipulate the price of gold. They profited, but many speculators were ruined. Even in modern times it's considered one of Wall Street's biggest scandals ever.

Library of Congress

Jay Gould

Why would Edison do business with Gould? Because Gould is only slightly worse than most other businessmen and speculators of his era. His biggest competitors, and the men who think they already own Edison's new device, are Cornelius Vanderbilt and his son William, who are every bit as ruthless as Gould, though somewhat more careful about appearances. As William will later say when someone warns him the public won't like a scheme he's planning, "The public be damned."

Gould and the Vanderbilts are battling over both of the new technologies of the era, the railroads and the telegraph networks. Gould, in addition to the several railroads, owns the Atlantic and Pacific Telegraph Company. Despite his frightening reputation, he's the underdog. The Vanderbilts own the country's best railroads and its largest telegraph Company, Western Union.

Edison knows all about that rivalry and about Gould's reputation. Shortly before the gold scandal,

Edison moved from Boston to New York, where financial companies have continued to be his best customers. This is part of a pattern that has continued through the Internet Age: People who buy and sell on the financial markets have always sought an advantage by getting news and price information sooner than their competitors. In the late 1700s, signal towers were built between New York City and Philadelphia, the two big financial markets in the colonies, to allow traders to profit from the price differences in the two cities. The financial companies of Edison's time need private telegraph lines and devices like Edison's specially designed gold price and stock price "tickers."

In focusing on these customers, and setting up private communication networks, Edison is doing exactly what large computer companies will do a century later in the 1960s. Years before the public signed on to the Internet, financial markets all over the world were exchanging price information electronically on private networks. The stock prices that run along the computer screens of modern investors would be perfectly familiar to Edison. Jay Gould too!

Unfortunately, what Wall Street giveth, Wall Street also taketh away. After benefiting from the economic boom that followed the Civil War, Edison was hurt by the bust in financial markets that occurred about a year before this meeting. He has continued to invent, but with so many traders out of business it's been harder to make ends meet. He's had trouble paying his employees, and has moved

Edison National Historic Site

An Edison stock ticker

his family from their house to a small apartment to save money. He's overdue in repaying some loans, and needs money fast. The head of Western Union gave him a small amount of money as an advance payment but left for a long business trip without closing the deal. Edison, a young man of twenty-seven with a fistful of problems, is too worried to wait. That's why he's meeting with Gould.

DOUBLE TIME

The device that Gould hopes to snatch from Western Union is the quadruplex telegraph, a machine that can send two messages and receive two messages all at the same time. This is a huge advance in telegraphy. A few years earlier the idea of just sending and receiving at the same time was considered impossible. How could a signal travel in one direction if another signal was coming the opposite way? It was widely assumed that the messages would become garbled. Then Edison came up with an ingenious solution: He sent two different types of signals along the wire, with machines built to distinguish one signal from the other. Now the quadruplex is another great leap forward. It'll allow much more traffic on the network. Combined with the other devices Edison has invented to automate the input, receiving, and printing of text messages, the company that owns the quadruplex will have a great advantage.

The idea of "multiplexing," as engineers call it, is important for any communication network, large or small. For example, on a single telephone call, multiplexing is the reason you can hear the person on the other end even while you're talking. The data can move in both directions at once.

A very sophisticated version of multiplexing called "packet switching" is what allows the Internet to work. In fact, it was the engineers who came up with it in the 1960s who built the first version of the modern Internet. They did it by working on the same kind of problem Edison was trying to solve a hundred years before. Edison's solution is obviously more limited, but it's still a huge leap forward.

CLOAK-AND-DAGGER

Edison has built a small network in his lab for the demonstration. As he shows the network to Gould, and talks about the circuits, relays, condensers, and other technical details, he can tell Gould doesn't know much about telegraphy. Gould seems to be relying on the advice of another man at the meeting, the owner of a telegraph company that's already using some of Edison's automated devices. All the devices work, but Gould doesn't seem excited by the demonstration. Edison is worried.

He doesn't need to be. In a few days, he'll follow a hidden passage in the basement of a Manhattan hotel to a concealed entrance to Gould's house next door, where another secret meeting will take place. Gould will pay Edison an astonishing sum for the rights to the quadruplex: $30,000 (more than $500,000 in today's money). Sweetening the deal for Edison is an

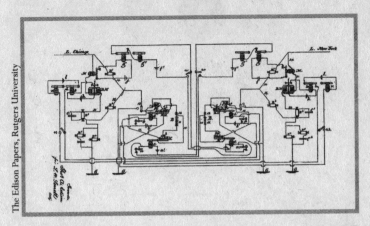

This diagram from one of Edison's patents reveals the complexity of the quadruplex. It shows a single line from Chicago to New York.

executive position in a new telegraph company Gould is creating. It'd be a great deal for anyone, and for a man with large debts it's a huge relief. After taking care of his accounts, there's more than enough left for what Edison has already planned as the next stage in his career: a large, independent invention workshop that has a ready supply of all the tools and materials he needs to pursue his work at the fast pace he likes. It'll be an idea factory—and some historians will call it his greatest invention of all. ❸

MENLO PARK

Raritan Township, New Jersey.

A short train ride from New York City is a lonely, unmarked New Jersey station, where a property developer's dream has gone wrong. Menlo Park was supposed to be a bedroom suburb of New York: close enough for businessmen to ride into town each morning and return to their families each night. It hasn't worked out that way. Instead of rows of houses, there are just over half a dozen. Most of the land remains unsold.

For Edison, that's perfect. There's plenty of room for employees but few distractions. It's too far from the city for his financial backers to drop by unannounced, yet so close to his customers there that he can see the towers of the unfinished Brooklyn Bridge and of Trinity Church at Wall Street and Broadway.

Using the money Jay Gould paid for the rights to the quadruplex telegraph, Edison bought a large home and enough land for a laboratory. Over the last few months, his father has been overseeing the lab's construction. Today is moving day.

Edison is waiting for his wife and two young children when the train pulls in for a very short stop. Their new home, a three-story house, is right across the street from the station. Behind it a windmill spins, and just beyond that is the laboratory. This is the building Edison cares about most. From the outside, it looks like a plain rectangular boardinghouse, two stories tall and about a hundred feet long. Inside, it's a marvel.

THE BOYS AND THEIR TOYS

The Menlo Park lab has the nineteenth-century equivalent of broadband Internet access: An amazing *twelve* telegraph lines run from the train station right into the lab.

The second floor of the lab, where the lines enter, is an open hall with several workbenches. This is where Edison and his lab employees—they're known as "the Boys"—perform their many experiments.

Edison has designed Menlo Park so he and the Boys are working inside a giant chemistry set and machine shop. Anything they might need is at hand. The shelves along the walls hold thousands of bottles, jars, boxes, and vials filled with exotic treasure. There are minerals, powders and liquids, like chloroform

Edison's home at Menlo Park. In the background at the right is the lab. To the left is the home of his chief assistant, Charles Batchelor.

and sulfuric acid. There are plants and seeds from all over the world—things like Brazilwood, Iceland moss, and even a bright red substance called "dragon's blood," which is derived from the sap of a South American tree and used in herbal medicine. Toward the rear of the room all kinds of metal, in both sheets and wire, are organized neatly. There's even gold and platinum. Edison boasts that "no substance that can be named" is missing from this vast collection.

The room contains several tables. One near the center of the room is covered with more than fifty large glass jars filled with acid and pieces of carbon and zinc. They're the batteries that provide the lab's electrical current. Wires run from them to the ceiling, and then to useful spots within the lab.

Other tables have tools such as microscopes, vacuum pumps, scales, spring-powered clockwork motors of various sizes, and large paper funnels for sound experiments. There is also plenty of electrical equipment: Automatic telegraph machines, electrical condensers that store charges, induction coils that concentrate the power of a current, and electric motors. In one corner sits Edison's personal table, where he handles his correspondence, some of which he can

> ALTHOUGH MENLO PARK, CALIFORNIA, IS ALSO KNOWN FOR ITS LINKS TO THE TECH INDUSTRY— GOOGLE IS ONE OF THE FIRMS FOUNDED THERE—IT WASN'T NAMED AFTER EDISON'S LAB. A RANCH AT THAT SPOT HAD THE NAME BEFORE EDISON MOVED TO MENLO PARK, NEW JERSEY.

send by telegraph right from here. Near the table stands a large pipe organ. It's here to be used for sound experiments, but Edison and the Boys often play it late at night.

Downstairs, an office occupies about half of the ground floor. Here Edison's personal secretary attends to business matters. The office also serves as the lab's library, and within glass display cases are many of Edison's early inventions, such as his gold and stock tickers. Among them is his very first patented invention, an electric vote recorder, which was meant to enable the House of Representatives to tally a vote in less than a minute instead of hours. That one was a flop. Edison built it before he spoke with his potential customers, the legisla-

> AUTOMAKER HENRY FORD ADMIRED EDISON SO MUCH THAT HE MADE A REPLICA OF THE MENLO PARK LAB TO SERVE AS A MUSEUM. SOME EQUIPMENT IN THE REPLICA WAS SALVAGED FROM THE ORIGINAL LAB. THE MUSEUM IS IN GREENFIELD VILLAGE IN DEARBORN, MICHIGAN.

tors. It turned out that they wanted a slow process so they'd have time to make deals and even change sides.

Further into the building a special table stands on two large brick pillars sunk deep into the ground to eliminate any vibrations that may interfere with the precise instruments used here. Wires connect the

Andrew Balet

Henry Ford's replica of Edison's Menlo Park laboratory even includes the pipe organ, visible against the back wall.

instruments on the table to the rest of the laboratory to make it easy to use the large, specialized instruments to test devices anywhere in the lab.

Then comes a large room filled with machinery and power tools. Pulleys and belts run between the machines and the ceiling so a large engine in the rear of the shop can power many of the tools at the same time. There are lathes, drill presses, and wood planers, along with precision tools capable of meeting the most exact specifications of Edison's designs.

Most important is the simple tool that sits at every worktable in the upstairs lab: a notebook. Because Edison's assistants perform so many experiments, they need to keep track of their results in a form they can share. Edison often reviews pages in an assistant's notebook and then makes notes for new experiments or designs the lab should try.

These assistants are technicians who had worked for him in New York and New Jersey before the move to Menlo Park. They have a variety of skills. One of

This photograph, though from a later Edison lab,
shows the heavy machinery in use at Menlo Park.

them deserves special mention: Charles Batchelor, a bit more than a year older than Edison, immigrated from England a few years earlier to help a company install large textile machines. That says a lot: Weaving technology is very complex. In fact, textile machines were the first kind of hardware to be run by "software." In the early 1700s, a French inventor devised a way to store weaving instructions on a series of paper punch cards. To make a specific design, a loom would "read" each card, one at a time, and move the threads automatically. (This system was the inspiration for the first mechanical computers, in the 1890s, which used paper punch cards for data storage; and punch cards continued

Library of Congress

Charles Batchelor

to be used for data and software storage as late as the 1980s, well into the electronic age!) Batchelor is bright and skilled, and soon after joining Edison's company in 1873 he became Edison's most trusted assistant and then his partner. They'll stay together for decades. They're a great team. They understand each other technically, and Batchelor's skill with engineering problems fits with Edison's instinct for coming up with ideas that seem impossible. Also, and maybe just as important, Batchelor doesn't mind staying in the shadows while Edison becomes "The Wizard of Menlo Park." **4**

CLEAR AS A BELL

Menlo Park, New Jersey.

If you spend enough time on the Internet, you're bound to run across a web page from the early days, before browsers included pictures and video and sound—before they even allowed different type sizes. It may even be a page from before browsers and hyperlinked text existed at all. For nearly twenty-five years, a page of text on the Internet was just that: a page of text.

Sound dull? It was.

You'd be dissatisfied with it, and maybe you'd be determined to make something better. By the 1870s, Edison and other inventors felt that way about their wired world. Just like the people building the modern Internet, nineteenth-century inventors were obsessed with finding the Next Big Thing.

On this day Edison has found it.

SOUND AND FURY

Several inventors have been trying to send sound over the wires that are now strung across the world. A few are already claiming to have done it. Not quite two years earlier Alexander Graham Bell spoke his famous words to his assistant, "Mr. Watson, come here. I want to see you." Before that, Elisha Gray had built a sound transmitter that wasn't clear enough for speech but was already being used to send telegraph signals more complex

Advanced office technology before the telephone: In the left foreground are "speaking tubes"—simple hollow tubes that ran to other rooms. Ships used these well into the twentieth century.

than the dots and dashes of Morse code. Both Bell and Gray were preceded by an Italian-born inventor named Antonio Meucci. Lawsuits have already been filed over the patents. (The controversy has continued into modern times. In 2002, the United States House of Representatives took the step of recognizing Meucci's work as the basis for Bell's.)

Whatever the device's origins, as of this day in 1877 Bell is the one who's credited with it. In the summer of 1876 Bell gave a demonstration at an exhibition celebrating the United States' 100th birthday. Among the spectators was Edison's assistant Edward Johnson. Johnson hurried back to Menlo Park to let Edison know about it.

While Johnson was enthusiastic, he had also seen the device's limitations. The sound quality wasn't

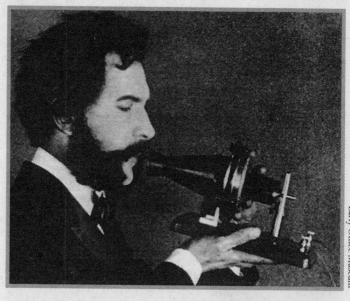

Alexander Graham Bell speaking into his telephone, 1876

good—yelling was often necessary—and the signal couldn't travel long distances. The Western Union telegraph company had already turned down a chance to buy Bell's patent. The executives thought it was a toy. They were more interested in using sound the way Elisha Gray's device was used: to create complex telegraph signals so several text messages could be sent at the same time.

Edison also didn't think much of Bell's work, but he was open to the idea's potential. He knew it was the natural extension of the telegraph network. Text messages are fine, but people mostly communicate through speech.

He had already been working on the problem, though more along the lines of Elisha Gray. He was trying to make something that suited the complex needs of the telegraph companies. So far he could use tones to send eight messages at once—a great feat. He had a feeling that sending just a single voice down the wire would be easier. The technical problems were difficult, but, he correctly believed, his experience and knowledge gave him a real advantage over Bell.

BUSY SIGNALS

Bell's telephone worked by causing an electrical current to flow from the speaker's end of the telephone, the transmitter, to the listener's end, the receiver. Unfortunately, he'd designed it so that the strength of the signal came from the volume of the speaker's voice. That's why users often had to shout.

Edison came up with the idea of using a battery to provide a current on the line that could then be altered just slightly by a person speaking in a regular voice. That small change made a big difference.

However, Edison still wasn't satisfied. The system was better, and could work over longer distances, but the sound still wasn't clear enough.

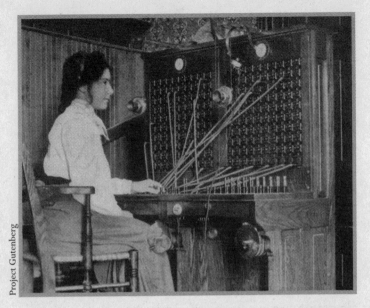

Numbers and dials weren't used on telephones for many years. To place a call you picked up the line and sent a signal to an operator in a switching station. The operator would pick up and ask for the name or number you were calling, then would put a wire into a plug to connect you. The photo above is a very small telephone exchange. A large city would have many rows of machines and operators.

Edison focuses on Bell's microphone as the problem. It's a container of electrically sensitive liquid (water and sulfuric acid) covered with a rubber diaphragm. The user talks at the diaphragm, and sound waves make the liquid vibrate. This moves a needle or wire in the liquid, which changes the strength of the device's electrical signal. Those changes are then converted from electricity back to sound at the other end of the telephone line.

Edison quickly decides a liquid microphone won't create a clear signal. Here's where his experience truly sets him apart. An experiment that failed a few years earlier gives him an idea. Back then, he had hoped to use pieces of carbon to change the strength of the electrical current in one of his devices. Unfortunately, the carbon didn't produce a constant result. The current changed whenever the carbon vibrated.

What was useless a few years earlier is perfect now. The vibrations from sound waves are enough to make carbon change the telephone current.

A quick test proves he was on the right track, but he's not satisfied. The sound still isn't good enough.

Carbon comes in many forms, and Edison is determined to test every variety and combination. The lab team tests a variety of carbon mixtures, mixing it with resins, gelatins, plaster of Paris, sugar, salt, and flour. Ironically, Edison's partial deafness may have improved his judgment in this case. It sets a higher standard. He certainly doesn't let it stop him. He tests some materials by putting a metal plate in his mouth to sense the quality of the vibrations made by the current.

The carbon that seems to work best is soot from kerosene lamps, also known as lampblack. Edison instructs the night watchman to gather lampblack from the lab's lamps each night. A shed is built on the Menlo Park grounds specifically for pressing it into the small "cakes" or "buttons" Edison wants to test.

BEFORE WORKING ON THE TELEPHONE, EDISON HAD A HIT WITH THE FIRST "COPIER." IT WAS AN "ELECTRIC PEN" THAT PIERCED HOLES IN A METAL PLATE TO MAKE A STENCIL. BEFORE THIS, THERE WAS NO WAY TO ECONOMICALLY PRINT SMALL QUANTITIES. THE ELECTRIC PEN IS STILL USED—FOR TATTOOS!

Refining the design has taken many more months, and a lot of frustrating trial and error, but he's sure he has it now. He instructs an assistant to use the lab's favorite test phrase, chosen because it has sounds that are hard to transmit well. The assistant says, "Physicists and sphinxes in majestical mists," into the transmitter. Edison is overwhelmed by the sound. Even better, when he cheers he can hear his own cheering come back over the line. The microphone, placed at the other side of the lab, has picked it up clearly. Later that day he writes to a friend—James MacKenzie, the man who helped teach him Morse code years earlier—"I've got it now without fail. Constant and good articulation with regular carbon but I work it on an entirely new principle. . . . I think it will work on any line without trouble from noise."

A few years from this breakthrough day, Edison's patent will be sold to the company that controls Bell's name. But while the nation's phone system will be associated with Bell, the carbon transmitter Edison has created will be the standard for more than a hundred years. Unscrew the mouthpiece of a phone from the 1980s and you'll find a carbon disk much like the ones Edison's lab assistants made by hand. It's still used in certain specialized telephones. Its design was also the basis of other kinds of microphones for decades.

Gerry Ashton

This carbon transmitter comes from a phone built around 1976—a century after Edison's first version. (Should you unwisely choose to remove the transmitter from a phone, the author urges you, based on personal experience, to replace it immediately rather than, say, taking it to school and losing it.)

But Edison isn't thinking about decades or centuries. On this very day he moves on to the *next* Next Big Thing. Having figured out how to transmit sound, he wants to capture it. ⑤

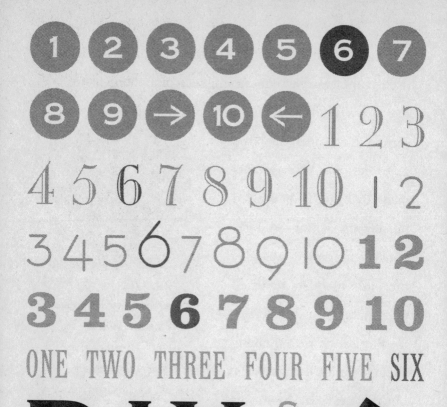

1 2 3 4 5 6 7

8 9 → 10 ← 1 2 3

4 5 6 7 8 9 10 1 2

3 4 5 6 7 8 9 10 12

3 4 5 6 7 8 9 10

ONE TWO THREE FOUR FIVE SIX

DAY ˢⁱ ˣ **6**

DECEMBER 7,

1877 **6**

EASY LISTENING

New York City.

Shocking but true: Once upon a primitive time, there were no portable music players. Music was live or it didn't exist at all. People didn't buy recordings of a popular song; they bought sheet music so they could play or sing the song themselves.

Then along came Edison.

At a time when most business correspondence (including his) was written by hand, he saw that the wired network of the nineteenth century needed voice mail and streaming audio. Then he set out to make them possible.

MESSAGE IN A BOTTLE

It's just over a week since the carbon transmitter triumph, and Edison is about to unveil a new invention. Right now he and some assistants are carrying it toward the offices of *Scientific American* magazine. They've been up all night testing it. They think it will work, but it's too new for them to be sure. Today will either be a triumph or a catastrophe.

A month earlier, one of Edison's assistants sent the magazine's editors a boastful announcement:

> . . . *Mr. Edison in the course of a series of extended experiments in the production of his speaking telephone, lately perfected, conceived the highly*

bold and original idea of recording the human voice upon a strip of paper, from which at any subsequent time it might be automatically re-delivered with all the vocal characteristics of the original speaker accurately reproduced. A speech delivered into the mouthpiece of this apparatus may fifty years hence—long after the original speaker is dead—be reproduced audibly to an audience with sufficient fidelity to make the voice easily recognizable by those who were familiar with the original. . . .

Unfortunately, at the time it was written, the letter wasn't accurate. There was no apparatus. Edison had the idea for it, but he'd been too busy with the telephone to build it. He didn't even begin until a week before this day, and quickly saw that his initial design wouldn't work well. But by then it was too late to back out. When *Scientific American* published the letter, the popular press jumped on it. Skeptical articles appeared in publications like the *New York Times*, which asked whether "bottled" speech would make reading and writing obsolete.

One reason for the doubts was Edison himself. Despite his reputation within the telegraphy world, the public hasn't heard much about him.

That'll change today.

TESTING . . . ONE . . . TWO . . . THREE

The "phonograph," as Edison calls it, was first imagined as a way to speed up the relaying of telegraph and telephone messages. Instead of using operators to repeat a message from station to station, the machine could do it. As usual, Edison was trying to automate the network.

About six months before this day, while he was in the middle of his telephone work, he played with the idea. His notes say:

Just tried experiment with a diaphragm having an embossing point and held against paraffin paper moving rapidly. The spkg. [speaking] vibrations are indented nicely and there is no doubt that I shall be able to store up & reproduce at any future time the voice perfectly.

While he was right to be confident, he was still far from his goal. He'd recorded sound, but not in a way that could be played back well. He didn't know this, because he didn't have time to test the new device properly. He was racing to finish his version of the telephone.

A few months later, perhaps in a moment of overconfidence, he'd allowed the letter announcing the phonograph to be sent to *Scientific American*. (That's why the letter referred to recording "upon a strip of paper," which isn't how the device he's demonstrating today works.)

> "PHONOGRAPH" COMES FROM THE GREEK WORDS MEANING "TO WRITE SOUND."

He still had a couple of weeks more work on the telephone before he could turn back to the phonograph.

Now that's he's working on it, another race is on—this time with his reputation at stake.

He soon discovers challenges. Playback is the biggest problem. "Paraffin" or waxed paper is great for recording because it's soft. The needle that's moved by the sound waves being recorded can easily scratch the pattern of those waves into wax. But for playback, a rigid material is required. The needle must follow the original pattern instead of cutting a new groove.

Another problem is the speed of the machine. If the machine doesn't turn at a constant speed, the recording sounds funny. A motor could provide a constant speed but it

EDISON HAD BEEN IN THE NEWSPAPERS BRIEFLY AFTER CLAIMING TO HAVE DISCOVERED A STRANGE NEW KIND OF ELECTRICITY. HE WAS DISMISSED AS A FOOL AND STOPPED HIS EXPERIMENTS. A COUPLE OF DECADES LATER SCIENTISTS REALIZED HE'D DISCOVERED RADIO WAVES!

would create vibrations, which would be recorded along with the sound waves.

Edison is clever enough to know that the phonograph isn't like the telephone: He just needs to demonstrate the principle, not perfection. He can compromise.

He quickly sketches an improved design. Now there's a brass cylinder, about the size of a large can of peaches, that sits sideways and can be rotated. To turn it, he decides to use a hand crank despite the lack of consistent speed. It's not how he'd want the public to use the machine, but it'll do for now. To replace the waxed paper, he has come up with the idea of thick tinfoil. He can cut a groove in it to record the sound waves, yet it's strong enough to control the needle on playback.

Library of Congress

The first phonograph

His machinist, John Kruesi, immediately sets to work on these new ideas. It takes six days for Kruesi to complete the first prototype. When it's ready, Edison and assistants gently stretch the tinfoil around the cylinder. Edison himself is going to give it the first trial run. First, all the machinery in the lab is turned off. Everyone gathers around and is perfectly silent.

Edison is careful to crank the machine at a steady pace, and to yell into the mouthpiece to make sure the needle vibrates with enough strength to cut a clear pattern in the tinfoil. Then he sets the needle back at the beginning and moves some parts so the sound from the needle will play through a funnel that will magnify it.

He turns the crank and the first human recording is heard: "Mary had a little lamb, its fleece was white as snow, and everywhere that Mary went her lamb was sure to go." Success!

Recalling this fateful night sometime later, Edison would remark, "[I] was never so taken aback in all my life. . . . I was always afraid of anything that worked the first time."

In the *Scientific American* offices, Edison removes the small crank handle from his pocket and attaches it to the phonograph. Cut into the tinfoil is a clever recording Edison has prepared especially for the editors. As the magazine will tell its readers, "The machine inquired as to our health, asked us how we liked the phonograph, informed us that it was very well, and bid us a cordial good night. These remarks were not only perfectly audible to ourselves, but to a dozen or more persons gathered around. . . ."

> **ALTHOUGH SOUND WAVES HAD BEEN "RECORDED" IN ONE OR TWO CASES PREVIOUSLY WITH MARKINGS ON PAPER, NO MACHINERY EXISTED FOR THEIR PLAYBACK.**

The editors would be even more astonished if they knew Edison had done most of the work on this device in less than a week!

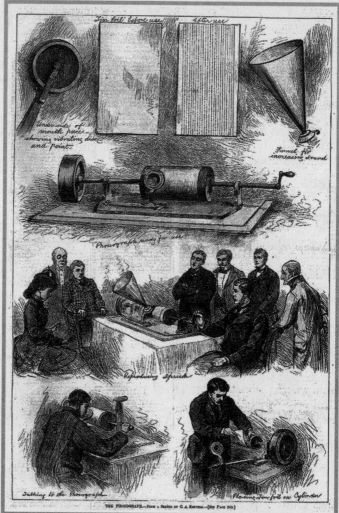

An illustration from Harper's Weekly *magazine of the amazing device. In the top center is the tinfoil sheet, before and after the recording groove is cut.*

THE WIZARD

The world is astonished by this invention—more so than by the telephone, it seems. Newspapers will give Edison nicknames like the "Napoleon of Invention" and the "Wizard of Menlo Park." The fame that comes from this day's demonstration will last a lifetime. From now on, all doors are open to him.

Ironically, this invention doesn't come close to meeting Edison's usual standards. Although he has the vision to predict all sorts of uses of it that will one day be real—recorded music, audio books, and even talking dolls—the current device just isn't good enough. The tinfoil recording is too fragile for the public to use, and the turning mechanism isn't simple enough. Edison, who has always prided himself on inventing machines with an immediate practical (and profitable!) use, has become world famous with something that doesn't work well outside of the lab.

Edison with an early phonograph

In fact it will take several years for most of the problems to be solved. (Turnabout is fair play: One of the inventors who improved it was Alexander Graham Bell!) When a good phonograph is finally made available, it will primarily be sold to phonograph parlors, where customers can record and play back their own voices. Edison will have to push his investors toward the idea of selling recorded music. That will happen in the 1890s, and it will be an immediate hit. A new industry will be created, and Edison will take the lead. He'll create a library of recordings so people will want to buy his phonographs. (That's the same business idea Sony will use when it creates the compact disk a century later. It will buy a whole record company to make sure recordings will be available in CD form. Apple, Inc. will also follow Edison's model when it launches iTunes. It wants digital music to be available so the public will buy iPod players.)

Library of Congress

The improved phonograph

Phonatic

A phonograph cylinder

In time, of course, answering machines and voice mail also became as common as Edison imagined. Streaming audio too. In fact, with a few clicks of your computer keyboard you can listen to some of Edison's earliest recordings streaming over the Internet, much like Edison envisioned back in the days of sheet music. **6**

Collection of René Rondeau

In 1890, when the phonograph is improved, Edison will briefly offer "Edison's Phonograph Doll, the Greatest Wonder of the Age: a French-jointed doll, reciting in a childish voice one of a number of well-known nursery rhymes." Either the technology isn't ready for the public or the public isn't ready for the technology or both. It doesn't sell. At left is the doll (22 inches tall) with phonograph mechanism removed. At right is a close-up of the miniature phonograph.

1 2 3 4 5 6 7
8 9 → 10 ←

1 2 3
4 5 6 7 8 9 10 1 2
3 4 5 6 7 8 9 10 **12**
3 4 5 6 7 8 9 10
ONE TWO THREE FOUR FIVE SIX

DAY SEVEN 7

DECEMBER 31,
1879 7

SWITCHED ON

Menlo Park. 4:39 P.M.

As the sun sets on this short winter day, there's more New Year's Eve excitement than usual in Edison's sleepy town. A crowd is gathering outside Edison's laboratory. The public has been drawn here by a newspaper story that promises an astonishing spectacle of electric light later this evening. Along with nearby residents are hundreds of people who have been arriving by train, not just today but over the last few days.

As the sky becomes dark, the town's gas street-lights are turned on and the good-natured chatter in the crowd becomes more serious. Stories about Edison's amazing invention, many of them inaccurate, have been leaking for weeks, and the people waiting in the cold for the midnight spectacular share them eagerly. There's a rumor that Edison's toughest critic, the respected engineering professor Henry Morton, is coming to see the demonstration for himself. Just the other day Morton denounced Edison in the *New York Times*. Edison promises a light that will be ten times stronger than a gas streetlight, but Morton believes it will at best merely equal a gaslight. Another rumor says a saboteur from a rival electric company is hidden in the crowd.

Inside the lab, only Edison is calm. His staff knows this demonstration is being rushed, and some wonder if it will work. His investors are worried too. Edison had already promised to illuminate all of the Menlo Park laboratory by the past October, and that didn't

Before the demonstration, the New York Times *was cautious.*

happen. They don't like the idea of betting the invention's reputation—and their investment—on a single, premature demonstration.

Edison has little choice. Earlier in the month, reporters and illustrators from the *New York Herald* spent two weeks in Edison's lab, drafting illustrations and preparing a big article to announce his advancements with his wonderful new invention. Then they printed the story earlier than Edison expected, a few days before Christmas. Since then the public and other newspapers have been trying to visit the lab to get a glimpse of the invention. Edison must move forward.

He may have been ushered into this moment before he'd planned, but he's determined to make good. Yesterday evening a crowd of some two hundred people had gathered in and around the lab. They'd heard a false rumor that Edison's great display would be that night. In good spirit, Edison gave the crowd a demonstration of what he calls "the different processes and experiments by means of which it is hoped a perfect electric light may ultimately be obtained." However, he didn't give them the final act of the show: He didn't reveal the lightbulb they'd all come to see.

THREADING THE NEEDLE

While the crowd outside is staring at the unlit streetlights, Edison stares at a single glowing bulb inside the laboratory. This handmade marvel has been burning fourteen hours a day for twenty-two straight days. In an age of giant machines—train locomotives, ship engines, gigantic steel-mill hammers—the most important invention of all has no moving parts. It's a product of Edison's intense laboratory method. Brain over brawn.

Edison's kind of light—the same light produced by regular lightbulbs today—is called incandescent, meaning the light is created because something is heated. But electric light already exists in other forms. Several months before the press descended on Edison, an inventor installed "arc" lighting in Cleveland. That system, based on a principle that was established in the early 1800s, makes an electric current jump or "arc" from one electrode to another. But arc light is blinding and can only be used in large spaces. Edison's incandescent light is better. It's subtle—more like gas lighting, only better because it burns more steadily. A week earlier some gas executives visited Menlo Park for a demonstration of Edison's bulbs and left scared out of their wits. Their profitable business, long established in public streets and private homes throughout the country, could go dark quickly.

Once Edison decided to take on the challenge of electric light—he didn't want the glory of that achievement to go to another inventor, and several are now testing possible versions—he and the Boys quickly broke down the job into a few problems that had to be solved.

The first was the creation of a good vacuum inside the bulb. Without a vacuum, air inside the bulb would make the filament burn so hot it would destroy itself. Edison's team solved this problem easily. They were skilled with machines and had all the right tools on hand. With quick experimentation, they settled on a good bulb design and perfected the vacuum method required for it.

The next problem was to regulate the flow of electricity. Too much electricity could also make a bulb burn out; too little would make it flicker uselessly. That was tougher, but it's what Edison and his team do best. They've been regulating electric current with telegraph devices for years. They know how to put together a complete working system. Edison makes sure that power supplied by his dynamos will match the needs of the lighting.

Finally there was the question of the filament: What material would burn bright but last a long time? Here the

JOSEPH SWAN, A BRITISH INVENTOR, IS SOMETIMES CREDITED WITH THE FIRST INCANDESCENT LIGHT SYSTEM. BUT AS SWAN SAID OF EDISON, "HE HAS SEEN FURTHER INTO THIS SUBJECT . . . AND FORESEEN AND PROVIDED FOR DETAILS THAT I DID NOT COMPREHEND, UNTIL I SAW HIS SYSTEM."

astonishing inventory of the Menlo Park lab gave Edison and his team an advantage no inventor could match. They were able to quickly try every substance they could imagine, from cardboard to platinum. When they found a substance that seemed to work, they then tried filaments of different shapes and thicknesses.

Two months ago they had tried more than a thousand variations and were exhausted when Edison himself chanced upon the answer. He was at his desk, lazily twisting a small piece of thin, black telegraph cord, when the cord twisted into a curlicue that vaguely resembled a horseshoe. Something about it struck Edison as right.

The team quickly tested the new shape with their favorite material, simple cotton thread that had been turned into carbon. The bulb lit up, but that was no surprise. Others filaments had reached this far, only to burn out. The question was, how many minutes would it last?

The team had asked the wrong question. They should have asked, "How many *days*?"

The bulb glowed for two days before Edison decided to test its limits by increasing the voltage and intentionally burning it out. As soon as the filament gave out, it was put under the microscope to reveal its secrets. They had their filament.

SPARK OF GENIUS

The last sunset of 1879 has ended. It's dark now. Edison gives the word, and the first guests enter the long laboratory building. The laboratory proper is lit with twenty-five brightly shining lamps. The office and library are lit with eight. Outside, along the road in front of the building, twenty electric streetlights are glowing.

Edison calls the crowd's attention to the lightbulb he was examining a few moments ago. He tells them it

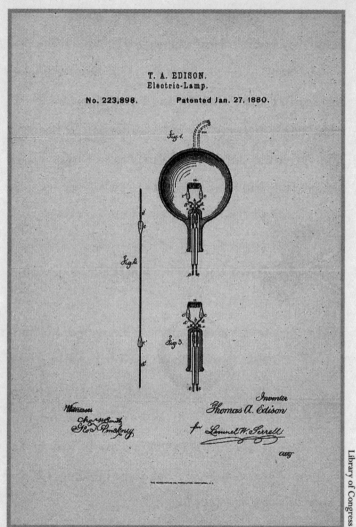

The technical drawing from Edison's patent application
for the incandescent lightbulb

has been burning fourteen hours a day for twenty-two days. The crowd leans in to see each bulb, wire, and dynamo. Edison doesn't mind revealing the techniques behind the magic. He knows that success depends on delivering a whole system, not just bulbs. Everything has to work together and be so simple that the public doesn't need to think about the mechanism behind it. "Our electricity will go from our central stations just as gas goes from the meter," he explains.

The height of the evening comes when Edison and his men display the lamps in a variety of tests, including placing the one bulb in a jar of water where it burns just as brightly as in dry air. "Wonderful!" the crowd exclaims, and Edison smiles to himself. The team also demonstrates a rapid turning on and off of his bulbs to show their durability.

By eight o'clock that evening, the lab is so crowded that Edison and his men have trouble moving from room to room. One woman gets a bit too close to a dynamo, and *zap!* the powerful magnets in the machine have pulled her hairpins from her head! Edison's team works hard to control the crowd, and make sure none of the machinery is damaged. Suddenly there's a scuffle. It turns out the rumor of a saboteur is true! A man from a rival lighting company is trying to burn out the system with strips of copper he'd been hiding under his coat. The police throw him out, and the special New Year's Eve party continues.

Not until noon the next day are the last stragglers sent home. Edison and his men take a moment to congratulate one another on a job well done. It's now 1880. Candlelight, oil lamps, gas lighting are all— well, they're all so 1879. The first year of Edison light has begun, and our world is suddenly a much brighter place. **7**

LIGHT THROWN ON A DARK SUBJECT.
(Which is bad for the Gas Companies.)

With the introduction of electric light, there was hope that gas
lighting companies, who were disliked because of high prices,
would be put of out business, and consumers would be free of
high prices. That didn't happen. Electric companies became as
unpopular as gas companies. In many cities and states, gas and
electric companies joined forces.

1 2 3 4 5 6 7

8 9 → 10 ← 1 2 3

4 5 6 7 8 9 10 1 2

3 4 5 6 7 8 9 10 **12**

3 4 5 6 7 8 9 10

ONE TWO THREE FOUR FIVE SIX

DAY

8

EIGHT

SEPTEMBER 4,

1882

8

FATHER OF PEARL

New York City.

I t has taken almost three years, but Edison, now thirty-five, is ready to unveil something that will amaze even New Yorkers, who are famous for thinking they've already seen it all.

Today's innovation shows the real difference between Edison and other inventors. He didn't stop after perfecting electric light. He has created an electric light *system*, taking into account all the practical difficulties that inventors in a lab usually leave to other engineers or later generations.

Today Edison will throw a switch to start six massive steam generators at a power plant on Pearl Street, which is near the base of Manhattan, not far from the Brooklyn Bridge and City Hall. If all goes well, those generators will convert that steam power into electricity, and the city that never sleeps will be lit all night.

Edison and his staff are making a careful last inspection of the facility and the equipment before he heads to the office of his chief investor, the millionaire J. P. Morgan. He has arranged to have the switch placed in Morgan's office, where Morgan and other financiers will be present.

Morgan is already a strong supporter of Edison's inventions. His home a few miles uptown is one of the few in the city equipped with electric lamps instead of gas for illumination. Edison has even installed a private generator for Morgan, to avoid the usual chemical batteries.

Edison isn't worried about failure today. He has

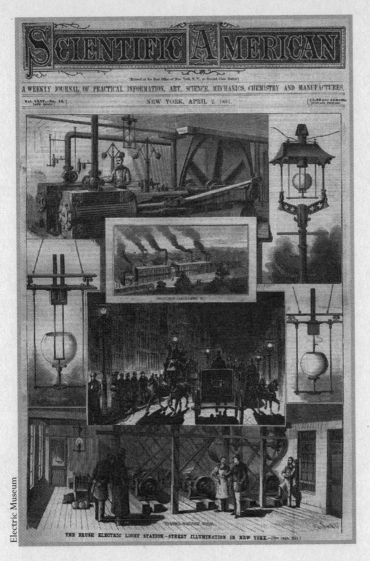

Edison's early competition: a rival power plant that provided arc lighting for public spaces, including New York's Broadway

already tested the system twice, once aboard a ship and the other time in London. He also limited his first effort to the downtown core so he could focus on getting it right before offering it to the rest of the country. Of course, attempting a project like this in the busiest part of New York is asking for trouble. It could have been completed more easily just about anywhere else. But Edison has his reasons for this location. This is the financial district, and he wants to impress the people whose money he'll need for expansion. The *New York Times* is also within the square mile his system covers. (It'll be another twenty years before the paper moves to Longacre Square at Forty-second Street, which will be renamed Times Square.) As usual, Edison is courting good publicity. He installed lights in the newspaper for free.

Edison's obsession with detail has served him well on this project. He started his design in a way modern business schools would admire: with careful market research. A house-by-house survey produced a complete picture of the district: the number of gas jets in the buildings, how many hours they burned, how much gas they used, and what each customer spent. Armed with this information, he calculated the amount of electrical power his generators must produce to properly service the customers, and what price would seem attractive.

Early on, Edison concluded that his wiring and cables should be underground, rather than strung on existing poles that carry telephone and telegraph wires. Adverse weather, occasional dangling wires and rickety installation of crossbeams convinced him he needed a more secure conduit for his cables. It took much persuasion and pressure on New York City's mayor and its other politicians before they agreed to let him dig beneath the city streets and plant his miles of wiring. Now there's one hundred thousand feet of cable—almost nineteen miles of it—running beneath this plant's range of one square mile.

As the concept of the system began to develop,

A dynamo at the Pearl Street Station

Edison and his staff at Menlo Park created the blueprints for each piece of equipment required. They've been awarded more than eighty new patents for their innovations, and dozens more are waiting approval.

Edison even had to invent a method for measuring his customer's usage so he could charge them accurately. He came up with a chemical solution that formed a coating on a metal strip when electricity was sent through it. By weighing the strip at the end of each month, Edison could translate the increase in weight from the added coating into a figure for how much electricity had been used.

Morgan was skeptical about the system at first, but when he used his own home as a test he discovered Edison's method almost exactly matched the records Morgan's employees kept by hand.

Always the salesman, Edison plans to manufacture and sell every piece of equipment in the system, including the lightbulbs. The Electric Light division of his company is already producing more than a thousand bulbs a day. Like a computer company that sells

A cutaway side-view model of the station, showing the dynamos that run the length of the building

music for less than it costs so people will buy its portable music players, Edison is keeping the price of the bulbs low so people will sign up for electricity service. In fact, the whole operation is expected to lose money for a while. Edison doesn't care. He envisions plants all over the world. In time, he figures, the cost of making the equipment and providing the service will come down.

At the offices of the *Times*, extensive arrangements have been made in anticipation of the test. In the editorial room, twenty-seven electric lamps hang beneath the extended bronze arm of existing gas fixtures. Another twenty-five lamps have been installed in the newspaper's business department. Each lamp has a thumbscrew. As the *Times* will later report, "To turn on the light nothing is required but to turn the thumbscrew: no matches are needed, no patent appliances. As soon as it is dark enough to need artificial light, you turn the thumbscrew and the light is there, with no nauseous smell, no flicker and no glare."

Creating the Pearl Street system took longer than expected. The New York Times reported on March 9, 1882 that customers were already losing patience.

There are about four hundred lamps on the system for this launch, spread over almost ninety customers. At every location, people are gathering.

When Edison is finally satisfied that everything at the Pearl Street station is ready to go, he walks to Morgan's office. He throws the switch at exactly 3:00 p.m., and back at the the Pearl Street station the massive dynamos—nicknamed "Jumbos"—begin to turn.

Because it's still daylight, the glow from the lamps disappoints some customers. The *Times* doesn't turn on its lamps for another hour or two, and even then the light looks dim. Some of the newsmen grumble. Then night falls.

"[A]bout seven o'clock, when it began to grow dark," the *Times* will later report, "the electric light really made itself known and showed how bright and steady it is. . . . It was a light that a man could sit down under and write for hours without the consciousness of having any artificial light about him."

Edison is justifiably proud of this accomplishment. To design a whole system like this, using parts that have to be designed as well, is an engineering triumph. Even more impressive is the fact that the system is made for the public rather than expert users. Edison has simplified everything for customers who think of electricity as coming from chemical batteries or noisy, expensive dynamos. The customer merely has to turn a switch. It's the same idea that Apple Computer's

Steve Jobs will follow a hundred years later when he's designing the first Macintosh.

The *Times* declares the system is a success. It plans to install another three or four hundred more lamps in the building, "enough to make every corner of it as bright as day." ❽

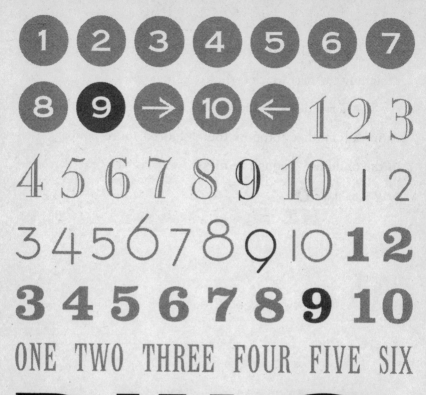

ONE TWO THREE FOUR FIVE SIX

DAY

NINE

9

AUGUST 6,

1890

THE HARD WAY

Auburn, New York. 5:00 A.M.

On an overcast dawn in this upstate town, twenty-seven dignitaries walk toward Auburn Prison. They're as somber as if they're going to a funeral. In fact, what they're about to witness is even more dreadful.

Around the prison, a massive crowd has gathered. It takes the men several minutes to move through the crowd to the prison gates.

The prison warden isn't there to greet the guests.

He's standing in front of the cell of condemned murderer William Kemmler.

"It's time, William," he says.

The warden reads Kemmler's death sentence. In a little while, Kemmler will be the first person to be executed with electricity.

Unfortunately, Kemmler's final hour is far from Edison's finest. Behind the scenes of the Kemmler drama is a business battle that has been called the "War of the Currents." A rival to Edison has appeared, with a new kind of electrical power. City and state governments are very interested in it. Edison thinks it's unsafe, and he wants to prove it.

When the State of New York asked Edison if electricity might be a more humane form of execution than hanging, Edison told them, sincerely, that the other system would be a good choice because its high voltages are deadly. He believes this, and there's some science behind it, but he also knows an execution would publicize the dangers of the other system.

CLASH OF THE TITANS

Edison, at forty-three the head of a large enterprise, is right to be concerned about the competition. He's being challenged by George Westinghouse, a smart businessman, who at the time is primarily known for inventing a clever railroad brake. (His basic design is still used today.)

The Westinghouse system is based on the work of a former Edison employee, Nikola Tesla, who is a true genius with electricity. When Tesla first immigrated

Library of Congress

George Westinghouse

to America from Europe he had a letter of introduction to Edison from Edison's trusted former assistant

Charles Batchelor: "I know two great men and you are one of them; the other is this young man!" Edison hired Tesla, but for many reasons, personal and professional, the two men didn't get along. To start, they have very different personalities. Edison likes to methodically test every imaginable solution to a problem, preferably with a team; Tesla likes to focus his thinking and solve complex problems all by himself. Edison devotes all energy to work; Tesla works hard but he also likes to play hard. Tesla also has a lot of opinions about the way to do things—ways that he believes are better than Edison's. That's not something Edison likes in an employee. Edison is used to employees who are an extension of himself.

Library of Congress

Nikola Tesla

It's an important part of his laboratory method. He's not the kind of manager who juggles competing egos.

However, this War of the Currents was really about science, not personalities. Tesla strongly believes that Edison's entire system of electricity needs to be scrapped. Edison's system, called direct current (DC), can be inefficient. When direct current is sent over a long distance, a lot of power is lost. Edison's power plants could only supply about one square mile. Tesla bluntly told Edison that the future of electricity is a new system called alternating current (AC). With that system, it's easy to increase power when the current is traveling over power lines, then reduce it when the current enters a home for lights or appliances.

Edison simply didn't want to hear this. Direct current was his baby. His companies made it and sold it. It was the basis of his fame. Tesla and Edison parted with bad feelings on both sides. (Among other problems, Tesla believed Edison cheated him regarding money. Edison had a different version of the story.)

By ignoring Tesla, Edison is making the greatest scientific mistake of his life—something he later acknowledged. The biggest business mistake too. AC is a much better system than DC for homes and offices. It's also better for investors, because it doesn't require so many expensive power plants.

This is when George Westinghouse steps in to finance Tesla's work. Westinghouse's support helps the reputation of the AC system, and AC soon becomes a serious rival to Edison's DC.

Edison's investors beg him to provide AC. But Edison has a different idea. Instead, he'll just scare people away from AC.

BLINDED BY THE LIGHT

Tesla has sometimes been labeled a "mad scientist" because of personal quirks. An example: Some of the most simple tasks had to be repeated three times—or some multiple of three times—because he was fixated on that number. At his regular table in the restaurant where he took many of his meals, the waiter was required to bring him eighteen napkins—three times six—which Tesla would then use to clean and polish his already clean plates, glasses, and silverware. (In our time, Tesla would be diagnosed with obsessive-compulsive disorder.)

Tesla's problems, while unfortunate for him, didn't harm anyone else. In the War of the Currents, it was Edison who developed a reputation for unreasonable behavior. Accusations of cruel animal experiments have been made against him.

The truth is more complicated. Edison believed that AC power was a bad system for the public because the power level is "stepped up" to dangerous levels for the long trips between power stations and homes. He was determined to prove to the public that AC was unsafe. It's impossible to say how much of his eagerness was based on his scientific beliefs, and how much was based on his business interests. The two were intertwined.

Soon after Westinghouse began to win contracts to provide AC power, New York State began to look for a more humane form of execution than hanging, which can take a long time to kill a person. This is when the state asked for Edision's advice. "Civilization, science and humanity demand a change," a government representative wrote to Edison. Could Edison help?

Edison replied that he would rather support "an effort to totally abolish capital punishment," but would help to at least guide the state toward "the most humane method available." He recommended the rival AC system, which he said could kill instantly.

While the state was considering his recommendation, Edison received a similar request from the American Society for the Prevention of Cruelty to Animals. At the time, animal control agencies put down animals by drowning them—obviously a painful and gruesome method. The ASPCA asked Edison if electrocution would eliminate suffering. Edison recommended it, telling the Society that it could probably use the same arc lighting devices that were already on the streets of New York and other cities.

This is when the animal experiments began.

Edison may deserve harsh judgment for the experiments. (Although other people actually performed the work, Edison was ultimately responsible.) There's

> INSTEAD OF THE WORD "ELECTROCUTION," SUGGESTED EDISON, PEOPLE SHOULD SAY "TO WESTINGHOUSE A MAN" OR "TO BE WESTINGHOUSED."

no doubt that publicity was mixed in with the science. Along with the experiments were public demonstrations meant solely to scare people away from AC. However, Edison and the others involved truly believed electrocution would reduce the suffering inflicted on the animals by existing methods. They were also sincerely worried that AC was causing a lot of deaths. About a year before this day's event at Auburn Prison, several deaths in New York City had led the mayor to order the shutoff of public arc lights, which ran on AC. He acted after a particularly awful incident right near City Hall. The *New York Times* reported,

. . . [M]*any persons who have to do with City Government were given a practical and never-to-be-forgotten illustration of the danger that lurks in the wires above ground. . . .* [A Western Union lineman fell] *across a network of wires which caught him across the throat and face and held him suspended some forty feet above the ground. The man appeared to be all on fire. Blue flames issued from his mouth and nostrils and sparks flew about his feet. Then blood began to to drop down from the body onto the pole, and a great pool formed on the sidewalk beneath. That* [the man] *was lifeless was apparent. There was no movement to the body as it hung in the fatal burning embrace of the wires. A great crowd of people collected and stood awe-stricken and fasci-*

nated by the fearful sight.

A lack of safety standards and political corruption were partly to blame, but the fact remained that AC presented dangers to the public.

A FLICK OF THE SWITCH

George Westinghouse is furious when he learns what Edison has concocted for Kemmler's execution. He hires lawyers who plead to judges that it will be inhumane, but he's unable to stop it.

So now William Kemmler is being led into the execution chamber. He sees a large wooden chair with leather restraining straps for his legs, arms, chest, and head. There's a metal plate that will be strapped to the top of his head, where a spot has been shaved bald.

Another metal plate will touch the base of his spine. One thousand volts will be sent from one of the metal plates to the other, through his body.

Rob Gallagher

The first electric chair

Two guards strap the prisoner into the chair. The room goes totally silent, and the signal is given for the event to begin. The electricity shoots through Kemmler and makes his muscles strain against the straps.

After just fifteen seconds, the execution is over and the current is switched off. The witnesses, who have been holding their breath during the horrible scene, exhale. Although it's been mercifully quick, they're staggered by what just happened.

Then as the guards remove the electrode from

Kemmler's head, a witness notices blood pulsing from a cut on Kemmler's hand. He's still alive!

"For God's sake," someone cries out, "turn it back on again!"

In the next chaotic moments, Kemmler seems to be regaining consciousness. His chest heaves. Then the voltage is doubled and the switch is thrown to let the power flow again. An odor of burning flesh and singed hair fills the room. A blue flame shoots out from the base of Kemmler's spine. After a few moments he seems dead, but no one is taking any chances this time. The electricity is left on for minutes. His brain is baked solid. Some of his blood looks like charcoal.

When the gruesome spectacle is reported, Westinghouse's AC system is spared the blame. As Westinghouse says, "They could have done better with an axe." Westinghouse will go on to bring Tesla's AC system to the public. Even Edison will switch his companies to AC eventually. With the right precautions it's a better system, and it's the one we use today. ❾

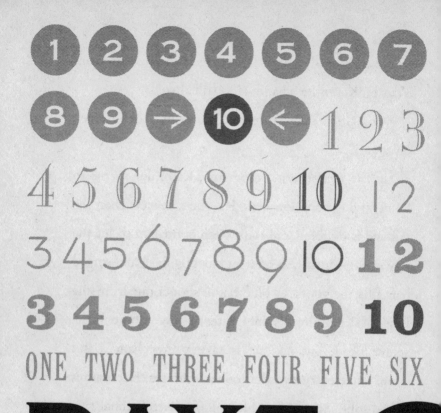

DAY 10

APRIL 23,
1896

TEN

LARGER THAN LIFE

New York City. 4:45 P.M.

In the balcony of a Broadway music hall, workers are scrambling over one another, hammers and wrenches in hand, to remodel the auditorium for a special performance. Red velvet seats are being removed from a section of the balcony, and carpenters are putting up walls to create a separate locked room.

This is the beginning of something important in history; but it also marks the end of an era for Edison. Although he has many years of inventing ahead of him—he's just forty-nine—this is the last time he'll unveil a world-changing innovation.

SPINNING HIS WHEELS

The invention that will have its premiere tonight is the large-screen motion picture. It's not wholly Edison's creation, nor did it come entirely from his workshop. But Edison's efforts have been a major force in bringing the movies to life.

Before Edison, the closest thing to a movie or video clip were children's toys. Images were painted along the edge of a disk that could be spun quickly to create the illusion of motion. A photographer named Eadweard Muybridge then came up with a way to take a lot of still photographs in quick succession, and placed those photographs on the same kind of disk. He'd created a real-life film animation.

About eight years before this evening, Muybridge was lecturing near Edison's lab and the two men met. Muybridge wanted to find a way to combine his device, which he called the "zoöpraxiscope" because his films were about animals and people, with Edison's phonograph. The audience would hear the sounds that should accompany the pictures.

Edison immediately saw the possibilities for video. There was also a mechanical simi-larity between the spinning disk of the zoöpraxiscope and the spinning cylinder of the phonograph. But Edison saw no need to work with

A zoöpraxiscope disk
(George Eastman House)

Muybridge, who hadn't come up with a new kind of animation. Any new device would have to be much different from the zoöpraxiscope or children's toys that preceded it, if for no other reason than the length of the video clip. Each phonograph cylinder contained about four minutes of music; each animation disk contained a few seconds of video. Solving that mechanical problem would require the work of Edison and his team.

Edison quickly sketched out a plan and filed a preliminary patent claim for "an instrument that should do for the eye what the phonograph does for the ear." He took charge of the mechanical problems—making a device that would produce the smooth, well-timed motion—and gave the photography problems to one of his best assistants, William Dickson, who already knew a lot about still photography.

First, Edison tried to arrange images on a cylinder, as he'd done with the phonograph, so the phonograph's reliable playback mechanism could be used. Then, on a trip to France, he saw a roll of photographic paper with a series of images on it. He was reminded of an old idea from telegraphy: a roll of paper that was moved through the device by gears that fit into sprocket holes. He drew a sketch for a devices

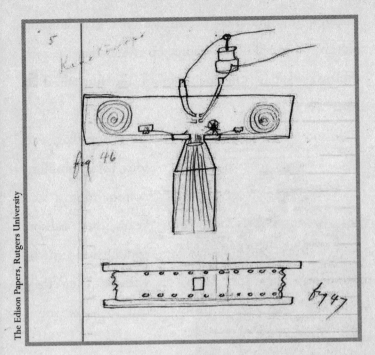

A drawing from Edison's notice to the U.S. Patent Office of a motion picture system using a roll of film with sprocket holes

that would move flexible photographic film the same way. It could be used within a camera to take the photographs and then within a device that would play back the film. The film itself didn't exist yet, but that wasn't a big problem. Edison would have it made.

Despite thousands of improvements in motion pictures since Edison came up with that design, Edison's idea is still the basis of the film used in Hollywood.

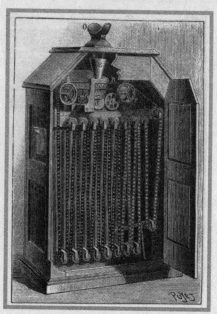

Library of Congress

Inside the player

From that one idea to a complete system took a few years, but Edison and Dickson stuck with it. Then they had to make some movies for the machine to show. Finally, about two years before this evening, everything was ready for the public. That premiere, however, was nothing like the one happening this evening. Watching Edison's new films was a lot more like watching video on a web page or a personal video player. Called kinetoscopes, from the Greek words meaning "to see motion," the short films were played on a viewer that looked like a large box with a peephole. The screen size was about the size of clips that show up on web pages or the screens of today's handheld games and video players. One person at a time looked through the peephole to watch the clip.

Library of Congress

This kinetoscope player included sound, and was known as the kinetophone. The customer is listening through earphones.

The size limitations didn't matter any more than the limitations of a handheld video player matter now. The public is instantly fascinated. Kinetoscope parlors are the video game arcades of the 1890s. They're full and profitable.

OUT OF FOCUS

Text messages, recorded sound, voice telephony, and video: By this time Edison has taken the lead in every kind of communication we consider essential today.

What was impossible, however, was keeping as much control over these media as Edison wanted. Competition in the nineteenth century was no less fierce than in modern business—if anything, it was more intense, because it was more difficult to enforce patents. Just as the film business instantly attracted viewers, it attracted a lot of people who were eager to make movie equipment and movies.

Two of these upstart competitors, brothers Gray and Otway Latham, have something in common with Edison: In the same way that young Edison could envision all sorts of possibilities for the primitive text-messaging network of his youth, the Lathams can see what's next for the film business. After making some

Early movie cameras were large and their lenses required a lot of light, so Edison and Dickson built a special studio. The building rested on a circular track (visible in the foreground above) and could be turned to capture direct sunlight. The studio was called the Black Maria because it vaguely resembled police vans with that nickname.

successful films, they start to work on changing the technology: They want to leave peephole video clips behind and instead project life-size images to a large audience. They think the public will be fascinated, and they'll be able to avoid the kinetoscope playback machines that Edison controls.

The Lathams are smart and bold. They offer a

partnership to Edison's assistant, William Dickson, who has been fighting with Edison about credit for the kine-toscope. It gives them the best technical mind in the business, which is just what they need to accomplish their new goal. He soon creates a system, and the partners have a little success. The images are dark and flicker too much, but it's a start. The audience likes it. Edison's investors are frightened.

> THE FIRST KINETOSCOPES OF EDISON, DICKSON, AND OTHERS ARE EASILY FOUND AND VIEWED ON THE INTERNET.

Edison tells reporters that the whole idea is ridic-ulous and the Lathams can't make it work anyway. Then, contradicting himself slightly, he takes up the challenge himself and promises to have a large-screen movie projector of his own in the next few months.

Edison's announcement changes the movie busi-ness instantly. Reporters, bankers, and even the public assume that when Edison's projector is ready it'll be the best. They've come to expect that of the Wizard of Menlo Park. (Westinghouse hasn't won the War of the Currents yet.) Investors are prepared to wait for Edison's version rather than put a lot of money into anything from a young company.

Unfortunately, Edison has nothing. Without his assistant Dickson, he has to start from scratch. The situation looks bad for him. Then, just like in a movie, a stranger rides into town to save the day. Some of Edison's financial backers are contacted by a young man named Thomas Armat, who has also invented a large-screen movie projector. Better yet, his already works well.

Armat is desperate for cash. For more than a year he has been trying to raise money to build his projector.

Library of Congress

Frames from "The Kiss," an 1896 film clip from Edison

He's already had a bad falling out with his coinventor. Edison's investors see a happy ending: Armat has a projector, Edison has a trusted name. Buddy movies have been made from less. Edison tweaks the design and gives the device a new name: the Vitascope, from the Greek meaning "to see life."

All that's left is tonight's premiere.

ACTION!

With a signal from Edison, the theater manager lets in the crowd. Everyone is staring at the screen. It's huge: twenty feet wide and twelve feet high.

The projectors themselves—there are two, so the audience doesn't have to wait while the films are changed—are hidden within the locked booth created earlier by the auditorium's crew. Edison doesn't want his competitors to copy the design.

Edison taps on the booth to signal Armat, who's inside. A loud whirring and grinding begins. The last

This early promotional poster for the Vitascope quoted from the New York Herald*'s review of this evening's premiere: "Wonderful is The Vitascope. Pictures life size and full of color. Makes a thrilling show."*

few theater lights are turned off. On the screen, a dull gray image suddenly turns into a dancing girl, almost exactly the size of a real person. For this occasion, the film has been colored by hand, so the image is vivid. The second film is a strongman flexing his muscles to thrill the audience. The crowd applauds. Now ocean waves are breaking on the screen. It's a close-up film of a beach scene. A large wave seems to hover above the crowd for a moment and then crashes down. It's so lifelike that people jump from their seats!

The crowd calls for Edison but he has already made his exit. He has an idea about making the projector better.

The man who lit the world has helped make magic in the dark. ❿

Library of Congress

Soon after the Vitascope was introduced, Edison devised his own projector, for which he used the well-known "kinetoscope" name. The advertisement above is meant for theater owners. The films listed can be found easily on the Internet.

1 2 3 4 5 6 7

8 9 → 10 ← 1 2 3

4 5 6 7 8 9 10 1 2

3 4 5 6 7 8 9 10 12

3 4 5 6 7 8 9 10

ONE TWO THREE FOUR FIVE SIX

AFTERWORD

OCTOBER 21,

1931

TRIBUTE

West Orange, New Jersey. 10:00 P.M.

Thousands of people have gathered at Edison's home and laboratory. Three days earlier, on October 18, 1931, Edison died. He was eighty-four years old, and had been active almost to the very end. He filed his last U.S. patent the previous January, shortly before his eighty-fourth birthday. It made a lifetime total of 1,093. The device was minor—something used to make metal parts—but it marked a record that no one has broken.

More than thirty years passed between Edison's last great innovation, motion pictures, and that final patent. In that time he shifted his attention from electricity and media. Although he continued to refine his earlier ideas and products, and to produce the "software" for them—recordings and films—he spent most of his time searching for innovations in mining and materials science.

The cement business, perhaps as mundane as the movies are glamorous, was just becoming a major industry. His innovations helped the industry to meet the new demands. The original Yankee Stadium was built with Edison cement!

Edison also tried to perfect dry-cell batteries. His goal was to improve the performance of the electric cars and trucks that existed at the time. Unfortunately, the 1908 introduction of the Model T by his good friend Henry Ford put an end to that dream. However, the batteries found many industrial uses.

His last great effort was to find a way to produce

Edison in about 1904, when he was in his late fifties. This photograph was taken in his second major laboratory, in West Orange, New Jersey. He'd moved there from Menlo Park in the late 1880s, and it remained his home until his death.

rubber from local, renewable plant resources. At the time, rubber, which was in great demand because of motor vehicles, was made from the sap of rubber trees. (It's now made from petroleum.) There were many political and economic reasons for the United States to avoid the countries and companies that controlled rubber production. Edison was on the right track—organic chemistry led to astonishing breakthroughs in the early twentieth century. Unfortunately, he never achieved his goal.

The great surprise is that he didn't pursue radio, which he had tried to create decades earlier as a way of transmitting text messages. At the

> WHEN EDISON WAS WORKING ON HIS BATTERY FOR ELECTRIC CARS, ABOUT ONE-QUARTER OF THE CARS SOLD IN THE UNITED STATES WERE ELECTRIC. A MODERN-DAY ELECTRIC CAR COMPANY HAS NAMED ITSELF AFTER EDISON'S RIVAL NIKOLA TESLA, IN PART BECAUSE IT USES AN ALTERNATING CURRENT MOTOR BASED ON A TESLA DESIGN.

time, he let the scientific community raise doubts in his own mind about his observation of radio waves.

Another remarkable device that other inventors pursued more vigorously was the vacuum tube. The building block of modern electronics, it's based on a principle, now called the "Edison effect," that Edison observed when perfecting the electric lightbulb. Edison did do some research on X-rays, which are created by one kind of vacuum tube, but halted it when one of his assistants, who frequently tested the

Edison in his late sixties, about 1914

X-ray generating tubes on himself, developed cancer and died. At the time no one knew that an overdose of X-ray radiation could lead to illness or death. Had Edison pursued safer vacuum tube research we might associate him with CRT televisions or early computers or microwave ovens. But sometimes it takes fresh eyes to see these things.

When Edison died the news was quickly sent all over the world—on telegraph lines that used Edison equipment. It reached the White House by way of a telephone call on a phone that used the Edison carbon transmitter. Tributes were prepared for newsreels, the weekly film reports played in movie theaters, which were created on film Edison had devised. Because movies had recently become talkies, those newsreels included history's oldest sound recordings: Edison's voice.

Now it's the evening of October 21. Thousands of mourners have visited Edison's casket at his laboratory in West Orange, New Jersey. The first lady, Lou Henry

Hoover, is one of them. She and Edison's family and closest friends have listened to a transmission of the public funeral service in a private room fitted with speakers—more Edison technology at work.

One last acknowledgment of Edison's accomplishments remains: at exactly 10 p.m. eastern standard time, at the request of President Herbert Hoover, lights across the nation are turned off and radio broadcasts go silent for one minute of remembrance. The darkness and silence are reminders of how Edison changed the world. ⟶

NOTES, RESOURCES, AND SELECTED BIBLIOGRAPHY

Baldwin, Neil. *Edison: Inventing the Century.* New York: Hyperion, 1995.

Dibner, Bern. *The Atlantic Cable.* Norwalk, CT: Burndy Library, 1959. http://www.sil.si.edu/digitalcollections/hst/atlantic-cable/

Dyer, Frank Lewis. *Edison: His Life and Inventions.* New York: Harper & Brothers, 1910.

Ford, Henry, with Samuel Crowther. *Edison as I Know Him.* New York: Cosmopolitan Book Corporation, 1930. E-book facsimile. Vancouver, British Columbia: Atomica Creative Group, 2006. http://www.atomicacreative.com/images/ACG_EdisonAsIKnowHim.pdf

Friedel, Robert D. and Paul Israel, with Bernard S. Finn. *Edison's Electric Light: Biography of an Invention.* New Brunswick, NJ: Rutgers University Press, 1987.

Israel, Paul. *Edison: A Life of Invention.* New York: John Wiley & Sons, 1998.

Jehl, Francis. *Menlo Park Reminiscences.* Dearborn, MI: Edison Institute, 1936.

Jenkins, Reese, et al, eds., *The Papers of Thomas A. Edison.* Baltimore: Johns Hopkins University Press, 1989.

Pretzer, William, ed., *Working at Inventing: Thomas A. Edison and the Menlo Park Experience.* Baltimore: Johns Hopkins University Press, 2002.

Robinson, David. *From Peep Show to Palace: The Birth of American Film.* New York: Columbia University Press, 1997.

Stross, Randall. *The Wizard of Menlo Park: How Thomas Alva Edison Invented the Modern World.* New York: Crown, 2007.

WEBSITES OF SPECIAL INTEREST:

Berner Machine Labs (Edison stock tickers by Klaus Berner)
http://bernermachine.com/

Early Office Museum
http://www.officemuseum.com/

Edison National Historic Site (National Park Service)
http://www.nps.gov/archive/edis/home.htm

The Edison Papers, Rutgers University
http://edison.rutgers.edu/

Edisonian Museum
http://www.edisonian.com/

Edison's Patents (chronological list)
http://edison.rutgers.edu/patents.htm

History of the Atlantic Cable & Undersea Communications (Bill Burns)
http://www.atlantic-cable.com/

Inventing Entertainment: The Motion Pictures and Sound Recordings of the Edison Companies (Library of Congress)
http://memory.loc.gov/ammem/edhtml/edhome.html

Metuchen Edison History (Jim Halpin)
http://www.jhalpin.com/metuchen/tae/taeindex.htm

Mr. Lincoln's T-Mails (website for book by Tom Wheeler)
http://www.mrlincolnstmails.com/

The Museum of Electricity (Charles Brush)
http://www.electricmuseum.com/

Phonozoic (Patrick Feaster)
http://www.phonozoic.net/

René Rondeau's Antique Phonograph Museum
http://members.aol.com/rondeau7/

The Telegraph Office
http://www.telegraph-office.com

The Telegrapher Web Page (Thomas Jepsen)
http://www.mindspring.com/~tjepsen/Teleg.html

Tinfoil.com (Glenn Sage)
http://www.tinfoil.com/

Who's Who of Victorian Cinema (Stephen Herbert, Luke McKernan)
http://www.victorian-cinema.net/

NOTES:

p. 4, "Genius": The precise origin of this quotation is unclear. It appeared in many obituaries in 1931, but may have first been spoken in 1900 or earlier.

p. 14, "t-mails": Tom Wheeler. *Mr. Lincoln's T-Mails: The Untold Story of How Abraham Lincoln Used the Telegraph to Win the Civil War.* (New York: HarperCollins, 2006.) See: http://www.mrlincolnstmails.com/

p. 27, "I've sailed": Israel, p. 32. From *The Papers of Thomas A. Edison,* Jenkins, Reese, et al, eds. (Baltimore: Johns Hopkins University Press, 1989.) vol. 1, p. 661.

p. 33, "Mr. T. A. Edison": *The Telegrapher,* January 30, 1869. Quoted in *Edison: His Life, His Work, His Genius.* William Adams Simonds. (Indianapolis: Bobbs-Merrill Company, 1934.) p. 69.

p. 37, "The public be damned": This famous remark was made on October 8, 1882, to John D. Sherman of the *Chicago Tribune*, and Clarence P. Dresser of the Metropolitan Press Bureau. *New York Times*, October 9, 1882, p. 1; October 13, 1882, p. 5.

p. 48, "no substance that can be named": "An Hour with Edison." *Scientific American.* July 13, 1878, p. 17.

p. 55, "The Wizard of Menlo Park": Edison was given this name by William Croffut of the *New York Daily Graphic.* "The Wizard of Menlo Park," *New York Daily Graphic*, April 10, 1878. The Edison Papers, Rutgers, Document ID: TAEM 94:158.

p. 66, "I've got it now": letter to James MacKenzie. The Edison Papers, Rutgers. Document ID: D7719ZDT; TAEM 14:1003.

p. 70, "Mr. Edison in the course": "A Wonderful Invention—Speech Capable of Indefinite Repetition from Automatic Records," *Scientific American*, November 17, 1877, p. 304.

p. 73, "Just tried experiment": Baldwin, p. 78-9.

p. 76, "[I] was never so taken aback": Baldwin, p. 83.

p. 77, "The machine inquired": "The Talking Phonograph," *Scientific American*, December 22, 1877, p. 384-5.

p. 79, "The Napoleon of Invention": A name supposedly given to Edison by the nineteenth-century actress Sarah Bernhardt. Edison was known to admire Napoleon Bonaparte, so someone may have given him that name before Bernhardt did.

p. 82, "Edison's Phonograph Doll": advertisement appearing as illustration on "René Rondeau's Antique Phonograph Museum" website, retrieved May 10, 2008: http://members.aol.com/rondeau7/

p. 87, "Edison's Electric Light" (newspaper clipping illustration): *New York Times*, December 28, 1879, p. 1.

p. 91, "He has seen further": Israel, p. 217.

p. 95, "Our electricity will go": "Edison's Electric Light; Conflicting Statements as to Its Utility. The Inventor Says He Has Succeeded in Getting a Cheap Substitute for Gas-Light A Public Exhibition Promised Prof. Morton's Criticisms." *New York Times*, December 28, 1879, p. 1.

p. 106, "To turn on the light": "Miscellaneous City News; Edison's Electric Light. The Times' Building Illuminated by Electricity." *New York Times*, September 5, 1882. p. 8.

p. 107, "The Edison Dark Lanterns" (newspaper clipping illustration): "The Edison Dark Lanterns.; The Company Unable to Say When the Lamps Can Be Lighted." *New York Times*, March 9, 1882. p. 8.

p. 108, "About seven o'clock": "Miscellaneous City News; Edison's Electric Light. The Times' Building Illuminated by Electricity." *New York Times*, September 5, 1882. p. 8.

p. 109: "enough to make": "Miscellaneous City News; Edison's Electric Light. The Times' Building Illuminated by Electricity." *New York Times*, September 5, 1882. p. 8.

p. 114, "I know two great men": Margaret Cheney. *Tesla: Man Out of Time*. (Englewood Cliffs, N.J.: Prentice-Hall, 1981.) p. 53.

p. 118, "Civilization, science and humanity": Israel, p. 328, quoting letter of Alfred Southwick to Edison, November 8 and December 5, 1887.

p. 118, "an effort to totally abolish": Israel, p. 328, quoting Edison's reply to Southwick, December 19, 1887.

p. 120, "[M]any persons": "Met Death in the Wires; Horrifying Spectacle on a Telegraph Pole." *New York Times*, October 12, 1889, p. 1.

p. 123, "For God's sake": "Far Worse Than Hanging—Kemmler's Death Proves an Awful Spectacle." *New York Times*, August 7, 1890, p. 1.

p. 123, "They could have": "Westinghouse Will Not Talk. But He Thinks His Claims Have Been Vindicated." *New York Herald*. August 7, 1890. p. 1.